ANCESTRAL DAUGHTER

ZEINA JHAISH

Published by
Daraja Press
https://darajapress.com

ISBN 978-1-998309-63-4 soft cover
ISBN 978-1-998309-64-1 ePub

Art Director: Tariq AlObaid
Cover designer: Sanad Hamdouna

Library and Archives Canada Cataloguing in Publication

Title: Ancestral daughter / Zeina Jhaish.
Other titles: Ancestral daughter (Compilation)
Names: Jhaish, Zeina, author.
Description: Includes some text in Arabic.
Identifiers: Canadiana (print) 20250296802 | Canadiana (ebook) 2025029933X | ISBN 9781998309634
(softcover) | ISBN 9781998309641 (EPUB)
Subjects: LCGFT: Poetry.
Classification: LCC PS8619.H35 A82 2025 | DDC C811/.6—dc23

EU Safety Information

Publisher: Daraja Press, PO BOX 99900 BM 735 664 Wakefield, QC J0X 0C2, Canada

info@darajapress.com | https://darajapress.com

EU Authorized GPSR Representative: Easy Access System Europe - Mustamäe tee 50, 10621 Tallinn, Estonia, gpsr.requests@easproject.com

For EU product safety concerns, please contact us at info@darajapress.com

TO ALL THE

PALESTINIAN
WOMEN AND
GIRLS
WORLDWIDE: YOU ARE MY COMPASS.

PEOPLE
IN GAZA
FIGHTING THE
UNBEARABLE
FIGHT: FREEDOM IS NEAR.

FREE PEOPLE
OF
PALESTINE: YOU ARE EVERYTHING TO ME.

ACKNOWLEDGEMENTS

Thank you to anyone who has ever inspired me with a word, a poem, or an experience. I am forever grateful for your presence, love, and support. Forgive me if I forget to mention you, I have been surrounded by countless important people, and I am grateful for my community.

Thank you to every peer who helped me with my writing (and spent so many hours on Docs with me). Thank you to every encouraging audience member at poetry events, to everyone who published my work, and to the poets I know for helping me grow.

Thank you to this book's first editor, Rawa Majdi, who has been my Palestinian writing inspiration from the beginning, and her and AJ's magic at Kuwait Poets Society, the beginning of it all.

Without Tariq AlObaid, the art director of this work, my poems would not be visually captivating the way they are now. He inspired me to envision what I care for you to see in this book. Thank you always.

To the illustrator of the cover, Sanad Hamdouna, thank you for your beautiful work. The book would be incomplete without you.

A special shoutout goes to Fatima Al-Jarman, the Editor-in-Chief at Unootha Magazine, who helped me develop in more ways than she knows. Thank you for teaching me so much, and for letting me teach you.

Thank you to my Gemini girlies at Sumou Mag: Jood, Tasneem, and Rania. Editing all of that magnificence with you will always be one of the greatest honors of my life. Thank you for being an unforgettable team and teaching me the joys of editing and relishing in other poetry and learning from others.

Thank you to Alana Dunlop and everyone who was with me at Mcsway McGill for always keeping me up with the poetry scene in Montreal.

Thank you to my family and my friends (especially Sara, Latifa, Karam, and Houda) who never let me doubt myself as a writer.

Thank you to my parents who listened to my poems before anyone else, and showed me that anything is possible.

Thank you for being the perfect parents to this ancestral daughter.

Thank you to my wonderful baby brother, you are the true inspiration behind it all.

Thank you to my great-grandfather and grandfather for instilling in all of us the love for literature.

To the greats and my favorite Arab women writers,
Suheir Hammad, Safia Elhillo, Randa Jarrar, and Susan Abulhawa, thank you for being a light in the darkest of times.

To all the writers in Gaza, the West Bank, and Occupied Palestine, my words are incomplete without yours, for they are rooted in your strength and wisdom. We must keep writing for Dr. Refaat, Hiba Abu Nada, Mohammed Abdulrahim Saleh, and countless others of our martyrs who fought with their pens and their poems. May they rest in eternal peace, and may we write the poetry of freedom soon.

Finally, to the love of my life,
thank you for being the final and most magical muse, habibi.

With endless love,
– Zeina.

شُكْراً

TABLE OF CONTENTS

TABLE OF CONTENTS

PROLOGUE

“Poem 7”

My first poem about Palestine,
January 15, 2010. Kuwait.

My Palestine changed

Palestine is my country

in my eyes it will remain

Palestine is my soul

Palestinian and proud

filled with history

Palestine the land of Al-Aqsa

thousands of years

our lives changed when they came

those who want to take it away from us

our love for our Palestine

our customs and traditions

those we share together

I love my dear country

Friday January 15
2010

Poem 7 قصيدة ٧

فلسطيني تغيرت
و
فلسطين وطني تراثي سوف تبقى
مليئ بالتاريخ و الأحداث
فلسطيني واقتي
فلسطيني بلدي
فلسطيني فيه المسجد الأقصى
موجود لآلاف السنين
وحياتنا تعيش معها
هؤلاء أن يأخذوه منا
حبنا لوطننا فلسطين
وعاداتنا وتقاليدنا
المشتركة بين بعضنا
أحب وطني العزيز

It is fitting as a Palestinian poet that one of the first poems I remember writing was about Palestine when I was ten years old. Today, I publish a book that reflects who I have grown into as a Palestinian woman.

At 16, I wrote a poem for an assignment and performed it in front of a crowd at a mall in Kuwait, making it my very first time performing poetry in front of anyone. At 17, I fell in love with poetry and saw myself becoming a performance poet, and since then, I never stopped. I performed a poem at an open mic about how (at the time), it had been six years since I visited Gaza. I performed at some more open mics. My goodbye to the poetry scene in Kuwait was one of the coolest moments I have had as a poet, where someone created a painting based on, actually, one of the poems in this book: "He."

Having since moved to Canada and joining Mcsway, I wanted to take poetry more seriously. I started publishing with different magazines (the biggest shoutout to Unootha Magazine, which believed in me enough to publish me multiple times and boosted my confidence as a poet in this cut-throat publishing industry). I joined Sumou Magazine as a poetry and prose editor. I completed a few writing programs and started becoming more experimental in my poetry, where I ultimately knew free-verse was my weapon of choice. I started performing poetry at protests and different open mics and events, writing a thesis about Palestinian poetry and its educational impact, and started submitting my poetry to more magazines. During the process, I relentlessly edited, added and removed from this book.

It has been my dream for almost a decade now to publish this book, and I pray that you love it as much as I do.

This book is who I am; an ancestral daughter, a daughter of Palestine, but also a daughter of life as it is.

Dimly lit room

beat-up notebook

fists wouldn't stop kissing the pages

I hide the books and the papers and the notes

in that broken drawer baba keeps fixing

My words

take the fall for me

in that beat-up notebook

in front of an ancestral desert

I talk to my brave papers

I start to believe

in my right to write

I learn that words are not voids, full as I

they survive the scratches

the crumples

the rip-ups

the cockling, warping into black and blue

I sit in my now brightly lit room

with my heart being written into what it needs to be

with what the world needs to see from me,

an ancestral daughter.

كلمـــــــــــــــــات
(What Words Have Made of Me)

PART ONE

ANCESTRAL

ONE.

THE BIRTH AND EXILE (OF AN ANCESTRAL DAUGHTER)

"The poised-tipped questions were shot at you: What will you write without exile? What will you write without the occupation? Exile is existence. The existing occupation is what hinders the efficacy of the imagination. I will write better."

– Mahmoud Darwish,
In the Presence of Absence
2006

My blood traces
back to a dystopia
with war and misery
check and
never-ending points

I am allowed
to be rooted
where I feel alright

What about time?
will I ever be calm
with my body?
will I ever be of one place?

I have written
about home
for as long
as I have been everywhere

My words are
coping mechanisms
for not being from
one earth
I lingered on one word
for days on end

Distorted ideas
of home
is what I know

This is the way
I begin
and I end.

A HOMAGE TO MY DIASPORIC MIND

REFRAIN

I refrain
from touching
my hair
I refrain
from remembering the origins
of my hair
my roots
to maintain
my heart
to keep it at bay
to maintain
its safety
and my legs walk
across another sea
to find other roots
my feet land
on a plant
crushed
there are no roots
there is no way
and I refrain from
watering up
an olive tree
I refrain from
touching my hair

(I refrain from going home where my hair used to grow).

On the bus I read poetry about home from a woman who lives in North America whose land was occupied too
and my writing continues to fall into irony as I ride on stolen land, too
seven in the morning, lucky morning, the dullness of it all bursting in full
I look up and Haifa is staring back at me
in the blurry orange display of this moving bus, this very rushed, very North American bus
Haifa feels like she does not belong
her name is enlisted on stolen land; she just wants to feel at home
Haifa tells me to come back and to stop being so cowardly

She asks me why her name is inscribed on the street sign before some 85th Avenue
she tells me that the streets in the North of Home do not look like those of here
asks me why everything looks the same
I tell her I do not like it either
with an everlasting sadness accompanying me
she asks again

Haifa, they took you away from us, you're stolen ground
they're honoring your colonizers here
they think you're someone else; I know better than that
she tells me I am not doing enough
she is throwing rubble rocks into my eyes
"Why did you leave?"

I was born in these suburbs
she asks me if I'm happy
I stay quiet
here they only thought Haifa was worth a street name
I promise her to come back

Haifa is made of the same mountain I am
I ride this very North American bus, lucky lucky lucky bus
I open my book and read poems about home from another woman like me
the everlasting sadness in her tone never leaves her, either.

HAIFA ON 85TH AVENUE[1]

GOD

FORS

H

AKEN

OMES

for I come into these same

God-forsaken homes

we once escaped from
two parts of me
molding into a mess
for I come from a home afar
to hold myself in another home here

I remind myself that heaven is a home
eternity keeps everything in one world where God awaits me

I wish I could write as if I had one place to be

And I am back with the blues of the oceans
I cannot see
and wonder if I can return to whatever one

God-forsaken place

I can call home.

TWO.

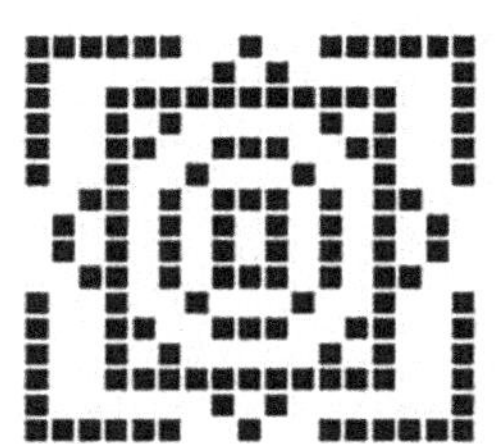

THE LAND (OF AN ANCESTRAL DAUGHTER)

”لن يُخلد الا من قاوم و قاتل وأما من تخاذل و خَذل فلن يذكره التاريخ و ستلعنه الكتب والمؤرخين عِش لما خلقت له و قاوم من اجله.“

“There will be no eternal legacy except to those who resisted and fought. As for those who betrayed, history will not remember them, and the books and historians will curse them. Live for what you were born for and resist for it.”

– Ahmed Ashoor Jhaish,
My father
October 2019

Familiarity escapes my arms
my hands become numb with nostalgia
I prickle with uncertainty, it will keep
consuming my body until the day my head
wraps around the phenomena that I will
always leave

homeland crosses into my heart with needles; my uncertainty stitched into courage

My fingers threading through the past and
courage will keep on consuming my body until
the day my head wraps around the dream that
I will always return.

TATREEZ[2] AS METAPHOR

MALFORMED MAPS

I
created a
map
to make sense of
where I should be
which place could
protect me
from the worst
things
that happened to
history I found
myself in places
where I am not
whole because we
could not create a
map that contained us

we are not cartographers

lost at sea in a bottle
with no directions
to where we belong
scratched by pens
that look like knives
that made the ink
on the map
that
misdirected
us
into
coming
here.

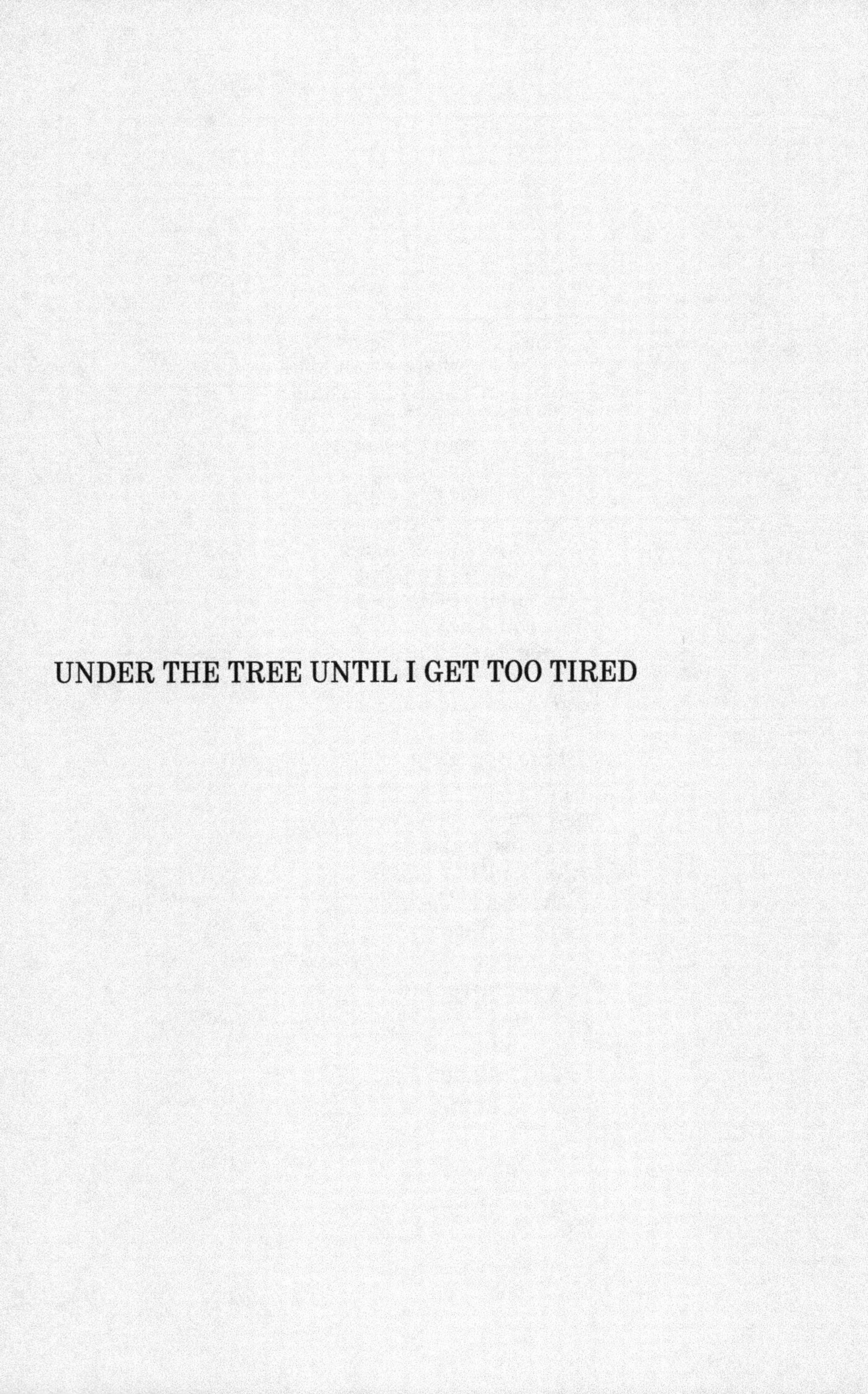

UNDER THE TREE UNTIL I GET TOO TIRED

to the settler sitting under my family's orange tree

I will not humanize myself for your sympathy; Perfect Victim[3]
but in reality your reality is my dream
I'm tired of acting like it is not existentially exhausting that my soul is not at home
sometimes I am tired of acting strong; that I am not tired of
imagining laying under the tree you stole forever
to the settler sitting under my family's orange tree
you have another home, and you will argue that I do, too, but you have not endured colonization you have not endured longing you are a thief
I can never find another home
I wish to pick olives from the trees I planted again under the living sun, the ones you eat now, you are a thief
until I get too tired
I want to scour the mountains, the ones you trek now
you are a thief
clean of colonization under the soft clouds
until I get too tired
I want to swim in these seas, the ones you relish in now
under the swaying moon
until I get too tired
I want to live at home, the one you're in now
cleaning it and adorning it with field-picked flowers, the ones you decorate your blood-stained hair with now until I get too tired
I will dream of lying under my orange tree, never too tired for what is meant to be.

My brothers long to smell the aroma of grape leaves floating in our air
to listen to our waves why then grace our settlement of a shore
they only hear the sounds of their delicate hearts inside of them break
as if heartbreak is their only destiny[4]
Their eyes emerald grass
growing and grounded
underneath the oppression wall[5]
eyes see home as the only end
my brothers are forced to be men[6]
picking flowers from the very soil that is malnourishing
them[7], each smile wider than the other, and I ask: how?

These are the green-eyed brothers I know

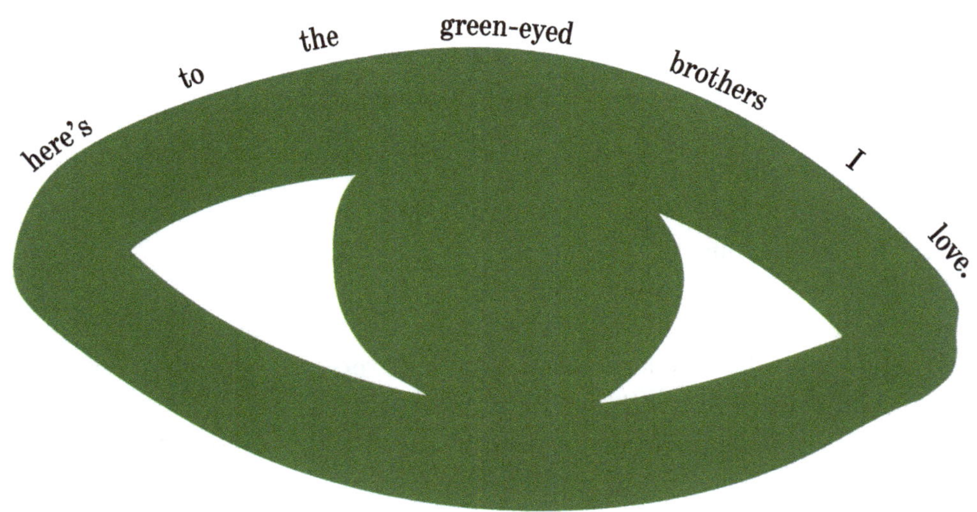

GREEN-EYED BROTHERS

MARTINI BLOODCLOUD

They stole my beaches and keep
fronting on the frontlines of the
sandlines[8] they build to tear my land
apart and I want them to feel the weight of what it means to steal my home
and it's between what I have never experienced
and all I have ever known you cannot club on stolen
land[9] you are not doing us a
service[10] you serve the likes of
hell and all we ever get are disservices
and I am tired of being nervous
about the next child that will
die when you sip your olive-garnished martinis on a cloud of blood, drenched
with the sweat of my people
tears from my
eyes coming to you all the way from
heaven how can you be full of
pride when you try to shame us into
oblivion how dare you have no
shame when you eat from our
land yet burn our olive
trees to the
ground on our
ground
driving us away
from being safe and sound
how dare you have no
shame when you bomb us away into shattered pieces painted with
melancholy and try to act with sympathy when you are dripping in evil
spitting on us with your bloodmoney hatemoney all from the brainwashing
you sprung across the seas as you skinnydip in our waters
try to foul play my
people but God is bigger than your
money how dare you have no
shame in front of the might
of the eyes of the Palestinian people.

They tell me I have complex trauma
around the same time I start to think that maybe I do
I realize a caterpillar can be murdered before it turns into a butterfly, when an enemy so vile can rip apart its cocoon
what is complex about murder?
I want to scream blood at the world machine manufacturing my trauma, they know exactly what they're doing
I sit away in my corner, far away from the scene, but never closer to the pain
I experience when a headline
is written to show an infant
who looked like me when I was younger, dead, shot in the stomach
when they tell me I have complex trauma my dreams redirect me back to the fact that every single part of me is hated on the land in which I come from
my dreams show me that a child was murdered this morning
I don't need to be awake to see it
I do have complex trauma because I woke up unable to breathe, I woke up feeling both chained on the sidewalk, chained in my bed, chained in my mind
I stay sharp when I'm awake because I don't want to slip, I don't want to fall, and I don't know (but I wish I knew) how to deal with complex trauma
I open my eyes and I wish I can whisper to myself that it was a nightmare
but it isn't, it was not, it will not be
the sun gently places its fingers underneath the blinds to lift the pain out of me
when I look right at the ground I see demolitions and fire
and when I look left at the ground I see murder and torture
I wake up on my side, wondering if they killed anyone
screams coming all the way from hell by the pending enemy-created monster in the back of my head
my blood traces back to the sun so I know I have complex trauma
when a man naturally loved by the same sun gets kicked to the sidewalk but is not chained rather obliterated by a bullet
& I stand and watch & cry
& I stand and watch & stare
& I stand and watch

OVER & AGAIN & OVER

then I stand and do something
& I feel a little better
then a woman who would look like me when I'm older is destroyed by the same bullet in the early morning of Friday
as I am going back to sleep
trying to be a butterfly, trying to have a peaceful, soundless life
trying not to delve into cliches when I am writing about my complex trauma
can't help but resort back to the cliches; they remind me that the world can be serene over & over again
but then my people are killed over & over again
over & over again
over & over again
I don't know where I'm supposed to go but into the arms of my people again
over & over again
over & over again
I sleep and I wake up over & over again
they tell me I have complex trauma, over & over again, without fixing the plant at the seed, without watering its leaves, without letting the butterfly see the sea, without letting it be, over & over again.

I sleep and I wake up over & over again I sleep and I wake up over & over a
& over again I sleep and I wake up over & over again I sleep and I
I sleep and I wake up over & over again I sleep and I wake up over & over a
& over again I sleep and I wake up over & over again I sleep and I
I sleep and I wake up over & over again I sleep and I wake up over & over a
& over again I sleep and I wake up over & over again I sleep and I
I sleep and I wake up over & over again I sleep and I wake up over & over a
& over again I sleep and I wake up over & over again I sleep and I
I sleep and I wake up over & over again I sleep and I wake up over & over a
& over again I sleep and I wake up over & over again I sleep and I
I sleep and I wake up over & over again I sleep and I wake up over & over a
& over again I sleep and I wake up over & over again I sleep and I
I sleep and I wake up over & over again I sleep and I wake up over & over a
& over again I sleep and I wake up over & over again I sleep and I
I sleep and I wake up over & over again I sleep and I wake up over & over a
& over again I sleep and I wake up over & over again I sleep and I
I sleep and I wake up over & over again I sleep and I wake up over & over a
& over again I sleep and I wake up over & over again I sleep and I
I sleep and I wake up over & over again I sleep and I wake up over & over a
& over again I sleep and I wake up over & over again I sleep and I
I sleep and I wake up over & over again I sleep and I wake up over & over a
& over again I sleep and I wake up over & over again I sleep and I
I sleep and I wake up over & over again I sleep and I wake up over & over a
& over again I sleep and I wake up over & over again I sleep and I
I sleep and I wake up over & over again I sleep and I wake up over & over a
& over again I sleep and I wake up over & over again I sleep and I
I sleep and I wake up over & over again I sleep and I wake up over & over a
& over again I sleep and I wake up over & over again I sleep and I
I sleep and I wake up over & over again I sleep and I wake up over & over a
& over again I sleep and I wake up over & over again I sleep and I
I sleep and I wake up over & over again I sleep and I wake up over & over a
& over again I sleep and I wake up over & over again I sleep and I

eep and I wake up over & over again I sleep and I wake up over & over again
p over & over again I sleep and I wake up over & over again I sleep
eep and I wake up over & over again I sleep and I wake up over & over again
p over & over again I sleep and I wake up over & over again I sleep
eep and I wake up over & over again I sleep and I wake up over & over again
p over & over again I sleep and I wake up over & over again I sleep
eep and I wake up over & over again I sleep and I wake up over & over again
p over & over again I sleep and I wake up over & over again I sleep
eep and I wake up over & over again I sleep and I wake up over & over again
p over & over again I sleep and I wake up over & over again I sleep
eep and I wake up over & over again I sleep and I wake up over & over again
p over & over again I sleep and I wake up over & over again I sleep
eep and I wake up over & over again I sleep and I wake up over & over again
p over & over again I sleep and I wake up over & over again I sleep
eep and I wake up over & over again I sleep and I wake up over & over again
p over & over again I sleep and I wake up over & over again I sleep
eep and I wake up over & over again I sleep and I wake up over & over again
p over & over again I sleep and I wake up over & over again I sleep
eep and I wake up over & over again I sleep and I wake up over & over again
p over & over again I sleep and I wake up over & over again I sleep
eep and I wake up over & over again I sleep and I wake up over & over again
p over & over again I sleep and I wake up over & over again I sleep
eep and I wake up over & over again I sleep and I wake up over & over again
p over & over again I sleep and I wake up over & over again I sleep
eep and I wake up over & over again I sleep and I wake up over & over again
p over & over again I sleep and I wake up over & over again I sleep
eep and I wake up over & over again I sleep and I wake up over & over again
p over & over again I sleep and I wake up over & over again I sleep
eep and I wake up over & over again I sleep and I wake up over & over again
p over & over again I sleep and I wake up over & over again I sleep
eep and I wake up over & over again I sleep and I wake up over & over again
p over & over again I sleep and I wake up over & over again I sleep

to the settler politician resting their feet on a couch in my village

you relentlessly have no regard for the sanctity of my entity
Sarafand Al-Amar[11] nor Palestine will ever be a territorial gain that your
bloodsucking ancestors mapped along with the devils Sykes and Picot
my people will never be property in sign-offs in your little game accords
where you hide behind buildings[12], hide behind your settlements

my soul is not a life you can just destroy under a war machine funded by your
friends, hiding in a white house where they also rest their feet on stolen land

hands off my home
g r e a t - g r a n d f a t h e r
painted the roof alone
our tangerines sense
your claws creeping

ripping roots of orange
as olive trees sob on sight;
murdering caregivers branched
on my land longer than you can
ever dream of thieving there

you try to break souls
and steal our worlds
kill off my neighbors and
family in Gaza with your toys
macheting tears away before
you move on to the next

hands off my home

weakness is not a trait I have, I pity
you, and the fire you try to burn
me with will only engulf your ways
pleasecontinuetobeintimidatedbythe
rocks I throw from Gaza to al-Daffeh

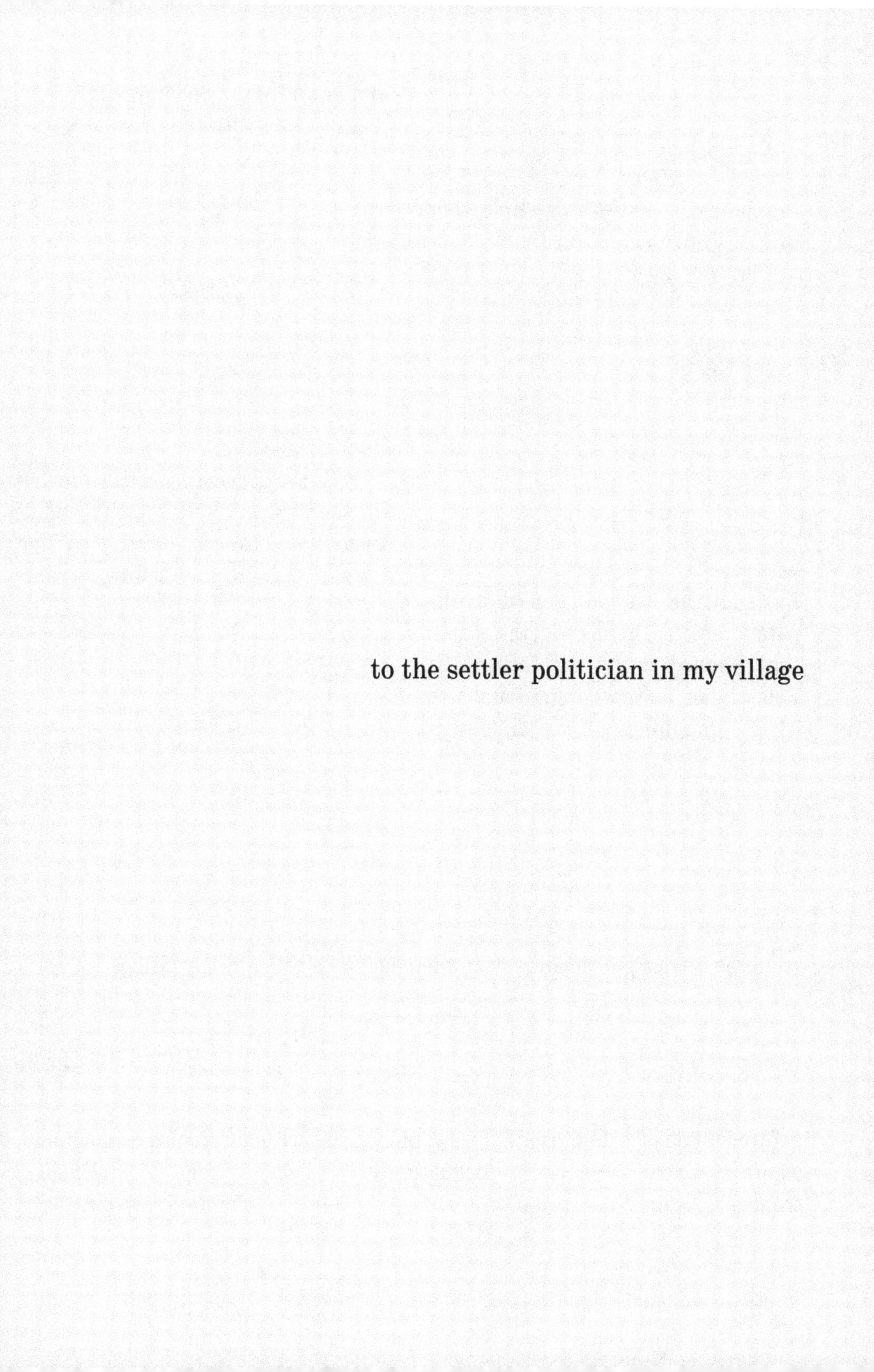

to the settler politician in my village

and know that my poetry will
disgrace you with the truth too;

the colony is a snake that will be chopped
in half by the son of a son of a son who
was murdered

in the Nakba

I trace the leaves my ancestors left
on the summer soil[13] in my village
under the sun that
burns your witching skin

I see all the answers I need in the
palms of the hands of the earth
that birthed me; I will always be
Palestinian, and so will the daughters
of the daughters of my daughters

so to the settler politician resting their feet on a couch in my village

hands off my home

before hell flashes its flames before your eyes, where your demise is inevitable,
where you will disgustingly beg for forgiveness
from the souls of our mercilessly-murdered

where eternal suffering will never leave you alone.

hands off

my home

THREE.

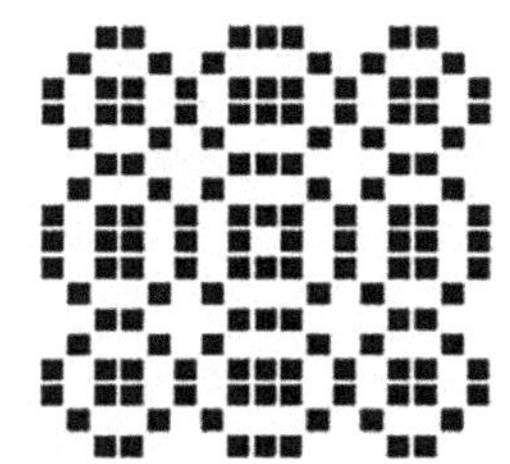

THE CITY (OF AN ANCESTRAL DAUGHTER)

“Patiently, we wrote out our history
And our honorable people, unphased
To the immortal memory of a loved one
His mother calling out for his return
Salutaions to Gaza, salutations to Gaza
To a great people as we bear witness
We have God.”

”كتبنا بصبرٍ حروفَ التاريخ
وما اهتز جِفنٌ لشعبِ الكِرام
لذكرى عزيزٍ مضى للخلود
تناديه أمٌ عَسَى أن يعود
سلامٌ لغزة سلامٌ سلام
لشعبٍ عظيمٍ ونحنُ الشهود
لنا الله.“

– Mohammed Assaf,
“Salam Le Gaza”
2024

Gaza
is a home
that is a
home that plays
a gruesome one-sided
game
where diseased olive and
orange trees reside
it is where peace
doomingly dies
occupiers beyond the
siege claim that it is
in our culture to be
pessimists[14] but how
can you blame us when
they stole the voice
that we laugh with

Gaza is a home
is a home where
the beaches are
polluted[15]
with the blood of
children who just
wanted to be, four[16]
(and more[17]) to be
exact the buildings
vanish with a trace
like the love and the
laughter on my streets

Bless our sand, legend sings
it's the only unstripped part
of soul we have left mixed with
the ashes of our dead people our
dying people
and the ones who are living
but are dead on the
inside.

STRIPPED

Gaza, 2003.

Every time I close my eyes

I watch Gaza's beach raging with a tsunami of blood

raging with the blood of brothers murdered

raging with the innocence of our kite-flying kids

raging with the tears of righteousness of Gaza's sons and daughters

Gaza's colors are those of gold & revolutionary red

I paint my body in its colors until I am taken away, too

I open my eyes to make room for my tears again & again

I am not done crying; my own tsunami

my thoughts land on both a maple and an olive tree

I am dimensions far from home

I cry enough to water all the trees

I close my eyes once more

my siblings cannot afford a change like I do

CRYING RAGE

I want to remember the good; I cannot survive otherwise

I relish in the far love of Gaza's glory

this time the most beautiful dream I will ever see

Gaza you are my forever safe haven

I wish to die on your soil

then the nightmares become more shaking than anything

& I cry myself to slumber another countless time

I question whether lives are cut short or if they were always short

I cry to Allah, only He knows the answers to my suffering

I close my eyes; Allah knows best

screams pierce my ears and I vomit tears

my family continues to run from terror

our horror is forever documented; I am forever scarred

in the heart of Gaza

every call feels like the last

every message feels like the last

every laugh feels like the last

every prayer feels like the last

I ache to survive

I remind my body nothing will be the last

nightmares seemed for sleepers

I am living a collective torment I cannot leave

every time I wake up, my body forgets that it still has a people

that it still has a family

I lift my body up in a frenzy

I frantically think everyone is killed

I begin my day by reminding myself that

the occupation has always snaked its way

into stealing so much light from me

I have never felt this much darkness

grandfathers staring into their killed daughters' eyes

on daughters sheltering siblings

on siblings wailing for their mother

on mothers' hysteria for their murdered sons

on sons' bloodshot eyes sobbing for the loss of their fathers

on fathers burying brothers

on brothers covered in their sisters' spilled blood

I cry endlessly for us all

a montage of pain slithers its way into me every time I close my eyes

my forearms shake trying to hold the rest of my body upright

a montage of longing, my family's faces run through my mind

each face is in a competition of remembrance

but how can I ever forget?

how can I forget that

the whole world is debating my pain

when I am the only one feeling it?

if it weren't for faith,

I would've drowned in a flood of agony

if it weren't for hope

I would've drowned in a self-made storm

if it weren't for love

I would've drowned in a natural disaster of neglect

if it weren't for Gaza gently placing me back on its ancestral shores

time and time again

I would've drowned in an abyss of forgottenness

I cry in rage and wait until my body is freed in the wake of liberation, where

I am empty of

nightmares, where I cry my final tsunami.

I NO
I NO
I NO
I NO
I NO
I NO
I NO
I NO
I NO
I NO
I NO
I NO
I NO
I NO
I NO
I NO
I NO
I NO
I HAVE NOWHERE ELSE
HAVE WHERE
HAVE WHERE
HAVE WHERE
HAVE WHERE
HAVE WHERE
HAVE WHERE
HAVE WHERE
HAVE WHERE
HAVE WHERE
HAVE WHERE
HAVE WHERE
HAVE WHERE
HAVE WHERE
HAVE WHERE
HAVE WHERE
HAVE WHERE
HAVE WHERE
HAVE WHERE
HAVE WHERE

I walk on this Earth, carrying Palestine in my palm

everywhere we offer her love and power

Palestine is the catalyst, is the liberation

the ground on which we will lie

I land in a land where everything I have ever known

is a mockingly short 6-hour drive away

I settled for tourism

way back when, settling was soothing, warm

never again, we are drowning in settlements

on a curbside street on an evening when I wish I were 6 hours away

I communicate my identity in stares, jokes, codes, and borders

friends' grandfathers fought many Octobers ago[18], and I walk somewhere

else

Visas only last so long

I have heard of the evils of dictatorship before I could even spell

Palestinians have always been accomplices to something; villainized

the Poetics and Politics of Palestine,

I must continue walking

In the desert I slightly rest

I can protest now, I would have never thought that I would see the day

I rode the same taxis I'd been taking for years

planted my feet by the beach, not mine, never mine

why would it be mine? I'm from another salty sea, you see?

In Amsterdam, I carry a blue passport with brown skin

the wind sadly gushes amongst the canals

I try my best to see how people do not think of colonization

all I felt were deep hypocrisies and useless apologies in Europe

the root of our displacement

In the desert I go back, I pray and I cry I pray and I cry

the light of our religion makes me want to forgive but I cannot

I pray on the concrete streets,

I feel small because I am

my forehead touches the asphalt; death is temporary

The first time a stranger kissed my cheek was in imperial America

a Mexican woman smiles at me with sorrow and love, "Victory is near, my dear"

I did not believe strangers and The Belly of Beast is ferociously hungry

I should have believed, pain can be spared, we make our own change

In Tunis an Amazigh woman tells me she knows Palestine well

a second kiss on my cheek, "We will pray in Al-Quds together"

I almost fully believe, her mothers know what it's like to break free

I sip tea in the desert and imagine myself doing so in mine

In so-called Canada I am transformative

here there is no room for mistakes, I cannot afford mistakes

here I am reliable, there are many enemies around us

a woman from Ecuador kisses my cheek, the third time

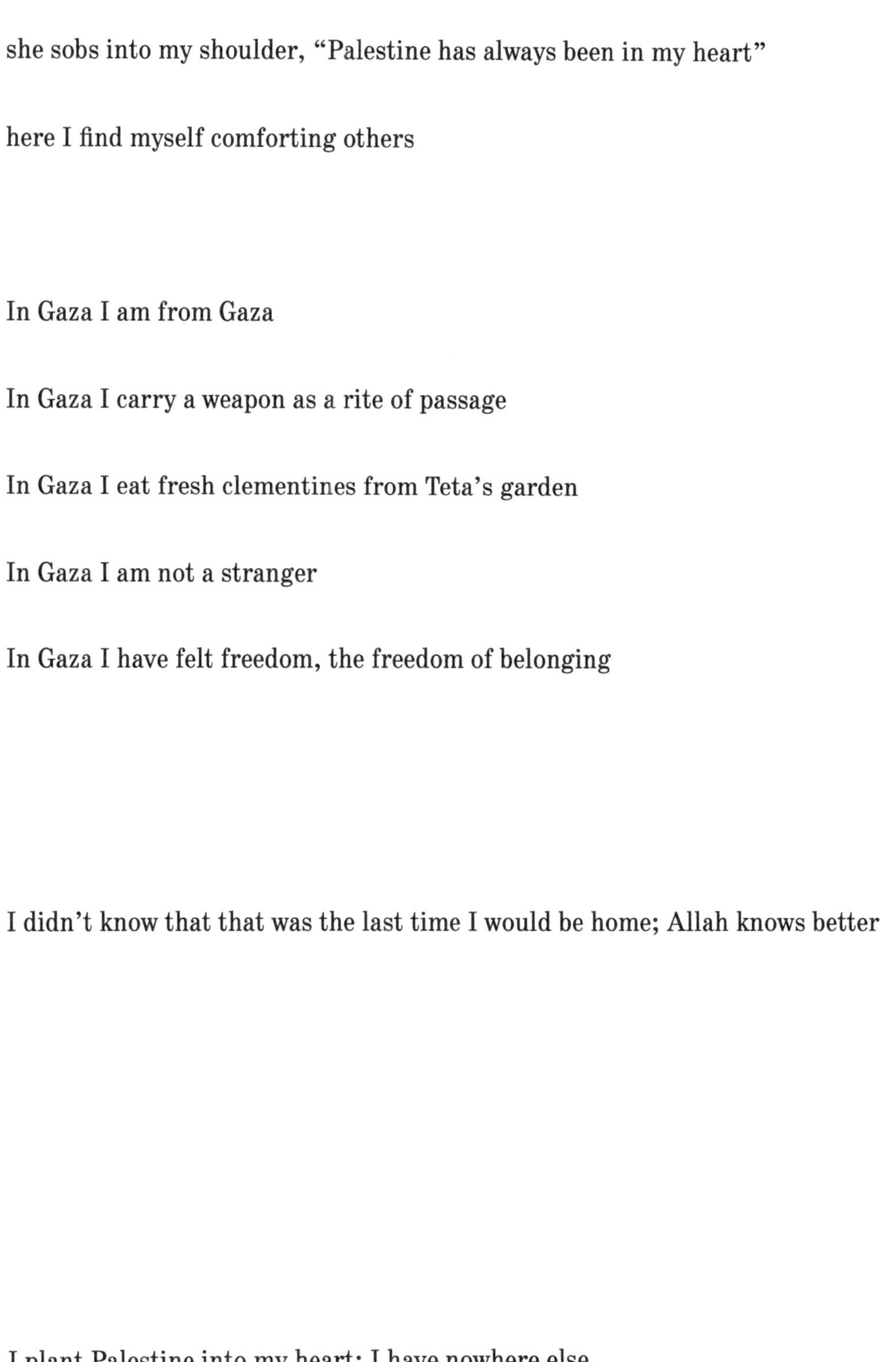

she sobs into my shoulder, "Palestine has always been in my heart"

here I find myself comforting others

In Gaza I am from Gaza

In Gaza I carry a weapon as a rite of passage

In Gaza I eat fresh clementines from Teta's garden

In Gaza I am not a stranger

In Gaza I have felt freedom, the freedom of belonging

I didn't know that that was the last time I would be home; Allah knows better

I plant Palestine into my heart; I have nowhere else.

Palestine the Purpose; my Pen-to-Paper
the breathing soul of every precipice of my existence
more than a mother, the compass of the cosmos
presence persisting long after we are all gone
I walk on an empty street and I dare it to lead me home
look down, my heart is raging with war and death
look up, my heart is flowing with love and dreams
I dare my body to continue running the same road
Ramleh Road was bloody 76 years ago, Rafah Road bloody now
Teta and Sido, Mama and Baba
they walked and walked for me to go back
village to city there and city there and city here
survivors of wars, of genocide, of others
on this day I am ripped apart
between pyrrhic pride for Palestine
and anguished grief for the gushes of Gaza
between rising in Intifada
and mourning the desecration of graveyards[19]
we are continually between pride and grief; how we continue running
between victory rallies and vicious realities
between a warcry and a wail
told not to dare dabke; my heart cannot survive plunging itself into pain
in my step there is a force ready to murder melancholy
told not to dare sing; my voice cannot survive killing itself with sorrow
in my voice there is a force ready to murder misery
I wrote and wrote to tell Teta and Sido, Mama and Baba that I will go back
I now pick up my pen to tell the paper and the people
to let it be known in front of the watchful gaze of history:
Gaza's grief is ours, stitched with its gauze
Gaza's greatness is ours, glamoured with its gallant
Palestine's pain is ours, perishing with prospects of liberation
Palestine's pride is ours, persevering with our martyrs' rejection of death
I will meet home in the soul, in the cosmos, in the glory of Gaza, and be long
gone under the flowering roads of Rafah.

TO MY GRANDFATHER AND THOSE IN GAZA'S GRAVES

ancestral daughter ancestral daughter

daughter ancestral daughter

ancestral daughter ancestral daughter

daughter ancestral daughter

ancestral daughter ancestral daughter

daughter ancestral daughter

ancestral daughter ancestral daughter

daughter ancestral daughter

ancestral daughter ancestral daughter

daughter ancestral daughter

ancestral daughter ancestral daughter

daughter ancestral daughter

ancestral daughter ancestral daughter

daughter ancestral daughter

ancestral daughter ancestral daughter

daughter ancestral daughter

ancestral daughter ancestral daughter

daughter ancestral daughter

ancestral daughter ancestral daughter

daughter ancestral daughter

ancestral daughter ancestral daughter

daughter ancestral daughter

ancestral daughter ancestral daughter

daughter ancestral daughter

ancestral daughter ancestral daughter

daughter ancestral daughter

ancestral daughter ancestral daughter

daughter ancestral daughter

ancestral daughter ancestral daughter

daughter ancestral daughter

ancestral daughter ancestral daughter

daughter ancestral daughter

Within a million nights

within a million and one days

in a world running on borrowed time, seconds vanish into unforgotten

history

I find myself under Gaza's sun

letting me bask in the light it creates for me

swirling in a pool of holy water

reminding me of the multifacetedness of righteousness

Gaza extends its resilience

its streets powerfully paint me into a bold exclamation mark dipped in

crimson blood

defines me in the same world that has already taken the decision

to shape me into a question mark

my Gaza was never of doubt

despite the dormant beast in me

Gaza remains, and reminds, to be gracious

flowering in every crevice of my soul

Gaza gave me a game plan of my place on this map,

not Gulf[20] or West, Gaza

was I born tired or did tiredness seep tauntingly into my body, both

days draw question marks onto my feet moreover & over

though, though, though

born strong, Mama walks with a lion's heart

how come I came out so full of Palestine?

Baba laughs, not a question

an eternal confirmation

he's proud, Gazan man

drives me to the border in the early morning

Baba's love living proof of Gaza

I am told by sons of home

that of Gaza I do not know

I refuse to let go, pre-devised enemy lines, inner battles and trying times

Gaza lets me lay my heart in its hands, what an honor to breathe in Gaza,

what an honor to be an ancestral daughter

clutching onto the love of Palestine's kids, my fingers clutch onto the left

side of the table at the ice cream place in Gaza City[21],

icy suburb mirrors remind me home is more than a mere reflection of history

smooth cold ice cream place mirrors recount to me that life fighting for

freedom is everlastingly sweet

Gaza my future, home lives, relive the joy, how tender

Teta's fingers draw resistance and exclamation marks into my hair

six in the morning, six birds sing in the garden of the mountain sons and daughters rush to greet the question-marked girl for the first time

I lay by Teta's cedar tree forever

I lay by Teta's lemon tree forever

ripe age of nine

nine and none more I know Gaza is mine

my body sits restlessly on a birthplace subway seat

my body sits steadily on a motorcycle in Rafah, my hair flies freely with

filled-in

crunched-in exclamation marks

Gaza knows freedom comes with steadfast love

eyes sit on a lake, I come from a lineage of land defenders

my eyes remain here then return to Gaza beach, body longs for a jellyfish

sting[22],

rolling in the sunset sand

my ears tremble in my aunt's house, I've heard rockets before I knew what

they were,

more question marks

but I know I left a girl from Gaza

ancestral daughter I am rising to let the world witness who I am writing an homage to my tears of gold to every breath of soul Gaza has gifted me

back rubs and healing tea

rooftop parties

rubble and no electricity[23]

living and running bravely

eating from teta's tree

surrounded by family

knowing your vile enemy

Gaza is greatly free

Gaza belongs to me

I do not succumb to misery

even after the last moment of my unforgotten history.

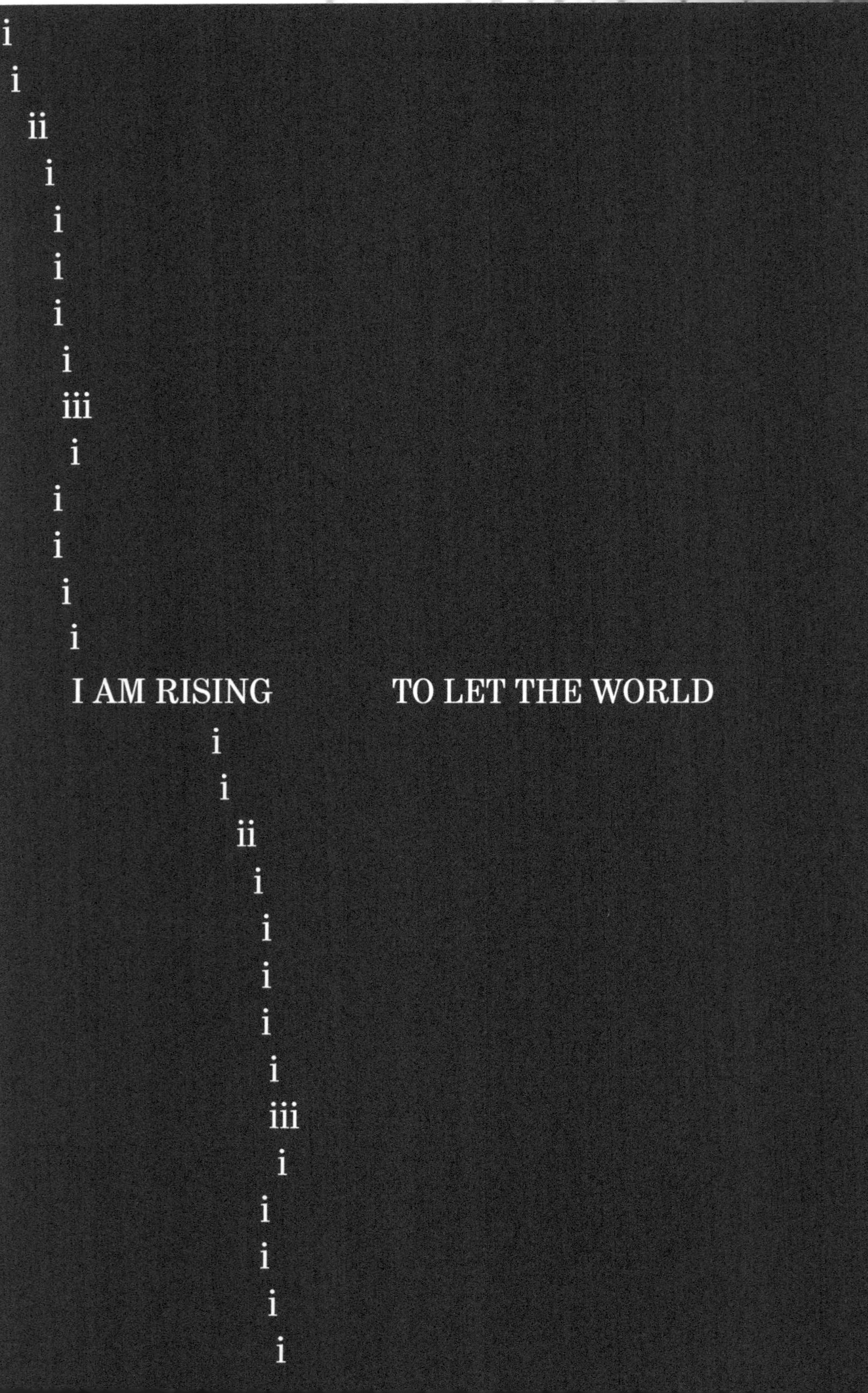
i
i
ii
i
i
i
i
i
iii
i
i
i
i
i
I AM RISING
TO LET THE WORLD
i
i
ii
i
i
i
i
i
iii
i
i
i
i
i

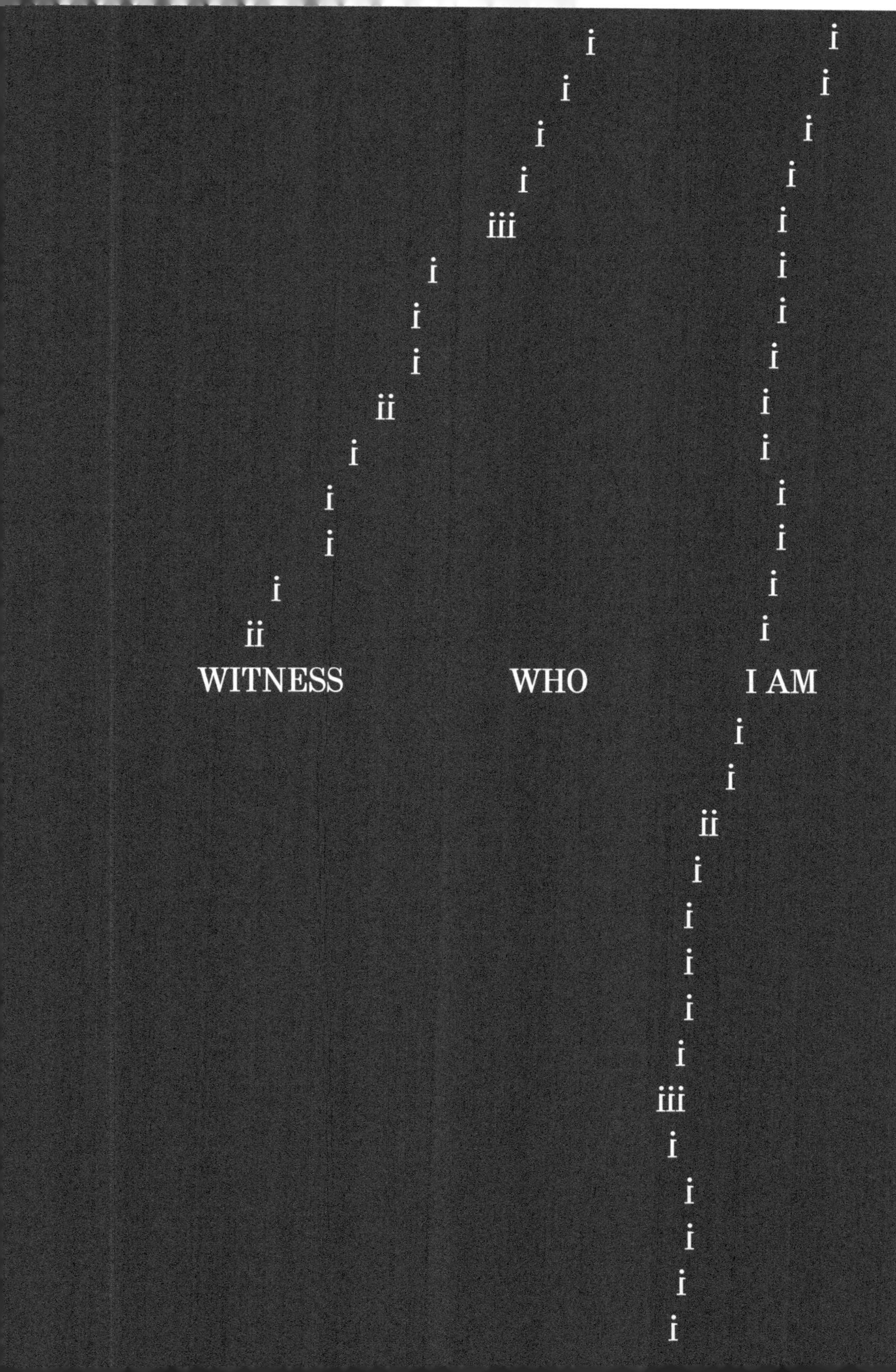
WITNESS
WHO
I AM

PART TWO

DAUGHTER

FOUR.

THE WOMANHOOD (OF AN ANCESTRAL DAUGHTER)

"Most of these women had ordinary lives, but life pulled the extraordinary out of them."

– Susan Abulhawa,
Against the Loveless World
2019

BEING A PALESTINIAN WOMAN: A GUIDE.

1. DON'T BE AFRAID TO TIE YOUR KUFFIYEH AROUND YOUR HEAD, STRENGTHENING THE KNOT UNTIL YOUR KNUCKLES TURN WHITE. YOU DESERVE TO BE ANGRY FOR ALL YOU'VE EVER BEEN WAS PATIENT, AND ALL YOU'VE EVER FELT WAS LOSS.

2. TALK OVER ALL THE MEN IN POLITICS; ONE WAY OR ANOTHER THEY'LL FIND A WAY TO SILENCE YOU. DO IT NOW BEFORE THEY TELL YOU IT WAS YOUR FAULT, TOO.

3. TELL YOURSELF HOW GREEN AND BRILLIANT YOUR EYES ARE, JUST LIKE THE OLIVE TREE SITTING OUTSIDE WAITING FOR YOU TO KNOW YOUR WORTH AND TO COME BACK HOME. YOU'RE THE ENTITY THAT KEEPS ON GIVING AND OUR WORLD IS NOTHING WITHOUT YOU BREATHING.

4. WEAR YOUR HEADPHONES AS YOU WALK DOWN A WAY TOO NARROW NORTH AMERICAN STREET AND LISTEN TO OUR MELODIES AND REMEMBER THAT YOUR SISTERS AND BROTHERS WILL NEVER GIVE UP ON YOU. TAP TO THE BEAT FOR YOU ARE ALWAYS OH SO FULL OF LIFE.

5. THEY'LL TRY TO BURN YOUR FLAG; TELL THEM IT'S FIREPROOF, AND SO ARE YOU, AS YOU DABKE AROUND THE FIRE THEY'RE FAILING TO MUSTER.

6. EAT FEWER BLACK OLIVES, I HEARD THEY MAKE THE BLACK HOLE IN YOUR CHEST EVEN BIGGER.

7, YOU'RE LUCKY TO LIVE THE STRUGGLE, EVEN IF YOU TELL YOURSELF A THOUSAND TIMES YOU'D RATHER BE FROM SOMEWHERE ELSE. I KNOW YOU FALL ASLEEP WITH A REVOLUTIONARY SMILE ON YOUR FACE.

8. REMIND YOURSELF THAT THE BLOOD YOU BLEED CAN NEVER STOP. THEY CANNOT TELL YOU YOU ARE NOT HERE.

9. RAISE YOUR SONS AND DAUGHTERS WITH THE SAME SMILE ON THEIR FACES. IT'S OKAY IF THEY HAVE THEIR EXISTENTIALLY SAD DAYS, TOO.

10. TAKE IT FROM ME, I'VE FELT LIKE A WALKING PARADOX GATHERED FROM A MILLION PLACES BEFORE. I'VE FELT HELPLESS BEFORE. I'VE FELT LIKE GROWTH WAS A FACADE CAUGHT IN AN ENDLESS LOOP OF LIES. BUT YOU ARE NOTHING BUT STRENGTH, AND THE BRIGHTEST OF SOULS REWRITE LIFE OVER AND OVER AGAIN BECAUSE OF WOMEN LIKE YOU.

Hair of an Heir

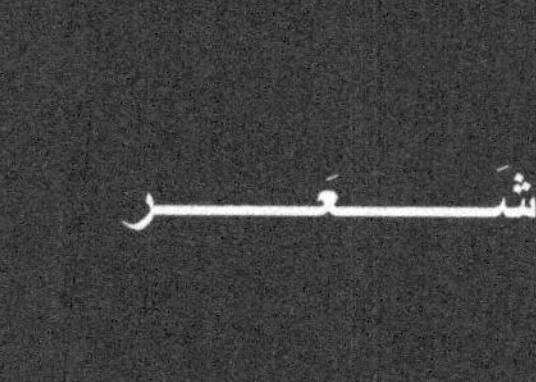
شَـــعَـــر

Flowers
are born out of
my body

poke each other on soft skin
I am more than what the paradigms tell me
I am

in remembrance of a grandmother whose roots
thrive from
thick, deep-rooted olive branches of the Holy Land

where soft leaves
f
a
l
l

o
f f
onto the smooth land

my body is home and land
I defend myself with these petaled thorns

my skin has been through
occupation, through freedom

my skin has been through disease, depression, and doom;
I have the hair of an heir of freedom and the desert.

AMETHYST

People rip me apart
paw at the royal purity in my heart
betray me and sell me for nothing
they try to disassemble my veins
and carve my corners
turn my reserves into melancholic blue
I put walls up to prevent an overflow of
deception
I wish I were protected by hard-cut glass
because I can’t be scraped
anymore.

Misplaced and put
everywhere
it's when I crave the ocean
and the moon overlooks my sorrow
that will is carried within me
as much as brokenness always will be.

INEVITABLE

SICK

Sometimes it's purely the way my fingers feel heavier than they actually are
about to let go of everything good they've ever touched
subsequently reminding me of when my legs betrayed me, heavy too
when doorknobs felt like I was twisting my fate
and walking felt like crawling the thinnest line this earth has to offer
I heard about the nimbleness and numbness of the heart and its delicacies
but no one damn told me that joints can break down my whole world and
restructure it all within one day and one night
and into what seems like forever
but I refuse to believe that pain lasts this long because
death is inevitable and so is the cure to my numbness

I picked up my bags and refused to let atoms tell me
how to live my life;
I infused so much love into my every breath
pills and pops later, cries
and doctor drop-bys later I got used to waiting in line
I got used to gut-wrenching days
after I burst into tears all the way through diagnoses in hopes that I can't
see the beginning of my journey
because of the constant blurriness; Oh Dear God
I cry often but what they do not tell you is that
I cry to live and I live to heal so here I am
a million days later feeling pain
but feeling ground-shaking strength
that I was once too afraid to feel
I overcame hurt and I overcame stigma
and I overcame the dryness in my eyes that did not come from the frequency
of my pain but the consequences of it
and I overcame the stairs that were too hard to climb down before they were
too hard to climb up
I overcame the alarm bells that made me more tired than alert they were
always within earshot and would feel like someone's shooting my lobes with
give-ups and let-downs

I remember the breakdowns in front of the world
with swipes of cards for bills
like cotton swab swipes like when I
was injected in my knees and in my back
and it felt like history repeating itself
but what they didn't tell me is that
I was born to handle pain; assigned at birth
numbness has nothing to do with me because I have always felt so alive
and I promise my bones that their home
is stronger than they are
who housed them after all?

I recovered into who I was,

I overcome the miles, with a smile.

FIVE.

THE HEARTBREAK (OF AN ANCESTRAL DAUGHTER)

"وسمعته وفكري شريد وسكت وقلبي شهيد"

"I heard him and my mind was distracted and
I was silent and my heart was a martyr"

– Samira Said
Al Gani Ba'ad Youmen
1981

he does not bother
with the universe's
complexities;

he believes him being one is enough
the world is ending now anyways

he lets go of reason

his love for her does not know how to fade; it
always comes for his heart
confusion fused with refusal
binding walls in his eyes;

he does not know how to look into the future

he lets go of the way

his lip trembles when

his entire entity shakes
when he loves her

he lets go of his life

he is in pain when I touch him

he remains a complexity

he is

he is the soil that catches
the last drop after a hurricane yet

he is the blinding sun
yet the furthest planet from it

he is between mercury and infinity

HE

he

he

he

he

is the bloodsucking
creature from the deepest trenches
but the lightest breeze caressing
the water

is a complexity when

loves her
and I become one too, when

loves her.

MELODIES ON THE BEACH

Waiting for a home for that one
song
I am trying to find a place for your
love
to find it in future
to find it in the patience
of writing melodies
that are scattered across the globe
I have looked in your eyes, for one
long long long time
the indefinite I played with
and the definite laughs
fate tells me I am too hopeful; I
put you on a pedestal shaped like
Atlantis but the feeling comes to
the composers
and music is found on the beach
we'll take the water with us
wipe our own droplets from the
creases of our eyes as the tide looks
at the moon
and tells you
I'm the one
across the oceans
the treble
the notes
we can discover the big blue
dance to our tune
and thank the ocean forever.

Come freely to set my heart on fire
on a cold summer day
for what is light without you looking for me
in the little truths you hide
behind your slightly cracked doors
in the ruins of the pavements
where we used to run away from ourselves
in the droplets of the sea calling out my name
in the specks of the sand calling out yours
in the light of the sunset calling us both
my veins went through the entire universe and its
elements to find you so come and send blood to my
heart, and free me from looking for you.

ELEMENTS

FAVORITE PART

The ocean speaks to me
across the nights
caressing me through the
navy in the sky
trying to reach me
like you do
it can never compare to
you
the ocean is a home that
can evaporate
when the world ends
I do not know where
it'll transcend
but sitting next to you
is my favorite place
the brown of your eyes
conversing with the waves
is all that it takes
a memory that won't fail
me
you will stay
when the ocean is gone
when the world has come
for our hearts
even if you forget my name
you'll know that you were
my favorite part.

I don't know whether it was the water its soothing whispers
or the wind trying to caress my hair when you were around
or the side-eye you used to give me
or that my blood traces back to the sun
I am missing the water and I am always missing your love of swimming
your inability to drown
or your inability to never make me forget
that I am always surrounded but
by nothing land

SWIM

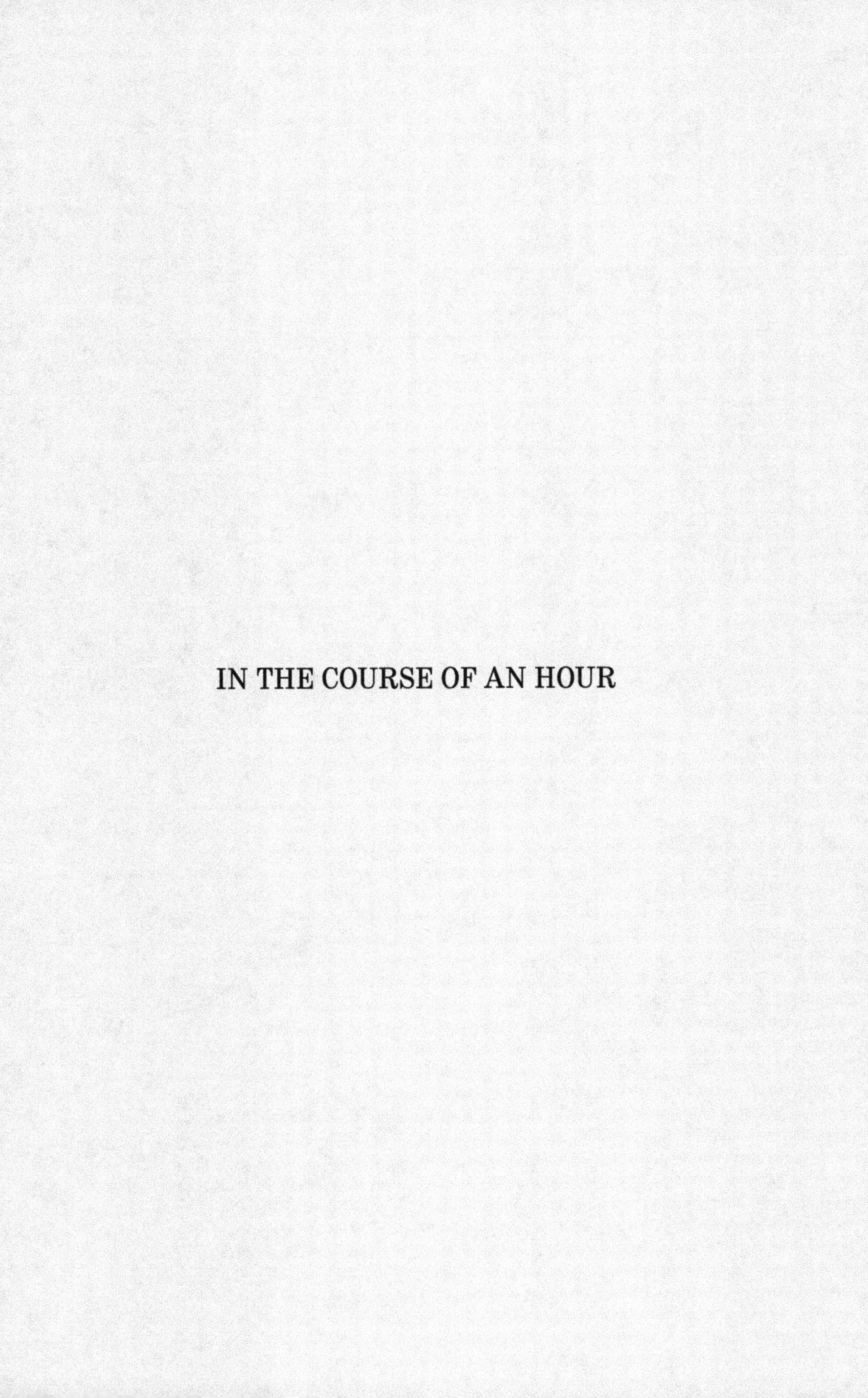

IN THE COURSE OF AN HOUR

BEFORE DAWN

We're back again to the tiringly timeless story of you and I
I call on myself to ask why I am void of sleep
to know why I am still in your sky while you are about to
somewhere other than mine
I tell myself I'm craving your palms surfacing my
hair

our
when we love each other now and in
you hold me
you break to make me smile
it's love
when you try to make our moons align when the
cosmos agreed
we should be gently placed
it's love

but then before I sleep at the tip of dawn
I know dishevelled and messy thoughts is what
you make of me
with loops of sleepless static calls and blurry
pixels
and I don't think you want to move towards me
even if it's love

but it's tiring that I can't seem to finish telling
the story
in the course of an hour

rise

impossible future

apart

before dawn.

ENERGIES

We are confidently parallels
when a million mountains
decided that we were
better off unmatched
I saw the bodies of water
between the buildings
agree that our beings
need to rehabilitate alone
the earth and its energy
redirected us to what was fate calling out our
names in different directions
and into scattered far ends
of time.

I told him that the night was frightening
"Do you see the stars?"
he told me that he adores her,
and hopes he will become with her love.

لقد قلت له إن الليل مخيفا
"هل ترى أنت النجوم؟"
قال نعم اعشقها
واتمنى ان اعيش بحبها و نكون

FAINT STARS / نجوم باهتة

SOLAR

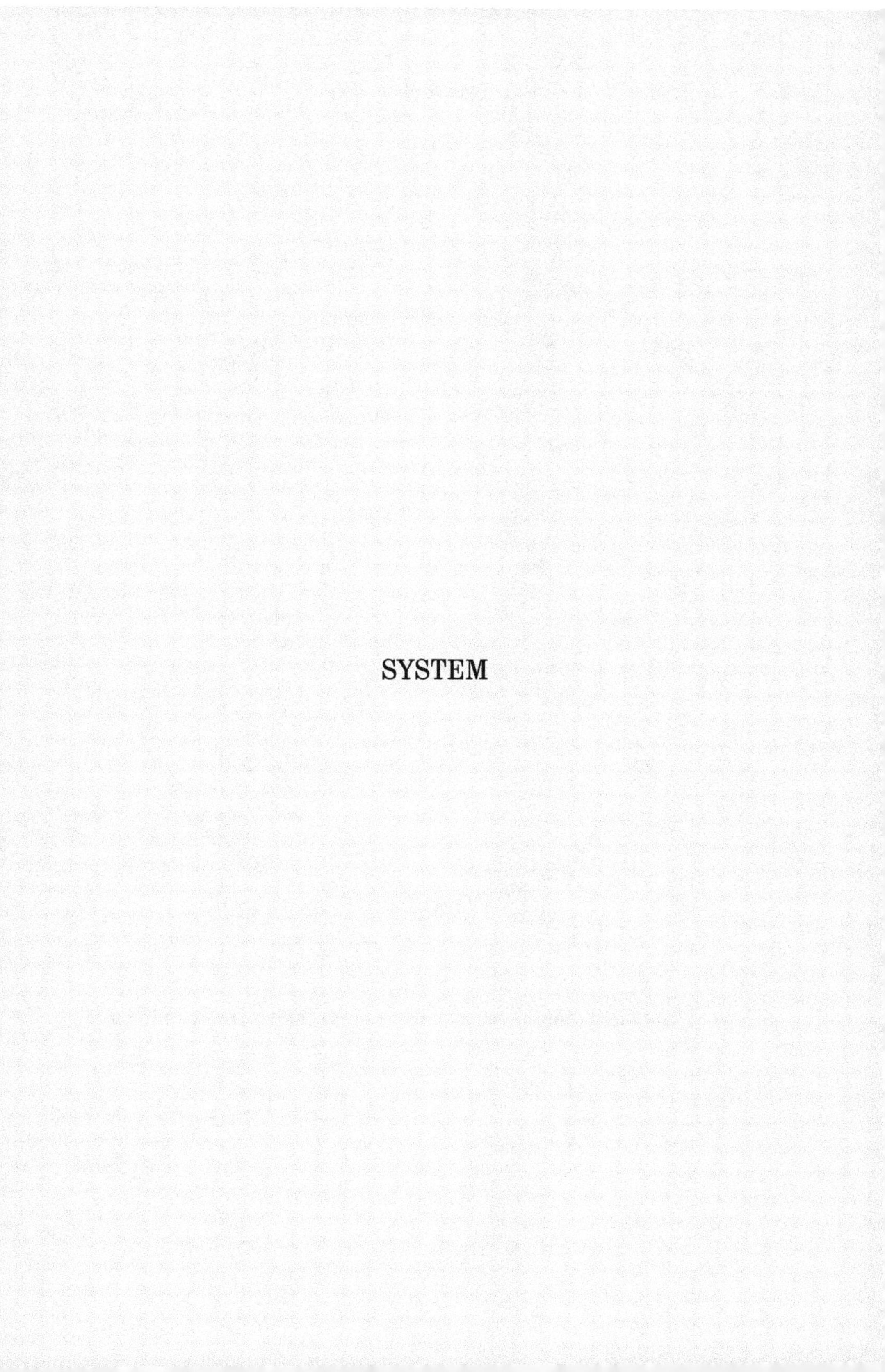

SYSTEM

The stars are stuttering

in disbelief that

the moon is making memories with another being of light

skip their jabs at them

the asteroids feel sorry for them

The black hole invites the stars and their sorrow in for a

l

r

i

w

s

but now I have come back to Earth
and I hope Venus gives you
the oh so solar light you were longing, lingering for.

NO SUN

My heart
helplessly shook
against its own cage
rapidly, carelessly
I memorized you again
for my mind
needs to remember
your ways on it
the space in the air
was too small for
both of our souls
but the sun shined for you through the dirty windows

the sun's lucky, you know?

She gets to see your grin the one I'll always
remember vividly
when I visit a place as warm as the one we grew up in
and I won't forget
my heart was crushed under yours
in a place as cold and gray
as the one you
left me in.

Every
stitched wound
dissolves
into my body
nicely,
intricately
as
I
think about you less
I
will never ever
go
back to the water
that
swallowed me whole

I
already
swam back to shore.

AFTER THE DIVE
(Swim Pt. 2)

-7 DEGREES

When your fingertips grace the sun
after they touched my skin in fake remorse
the snow freezes on the concrete, the
warmth spirals into the wind, the ice
becomes a flowerbed to everything cold
you have ever sprung upon my heart.

FLATLINE

SIX.

THE LOVE (OF AN ANCESTRAL DAUGHTER)

"Of all the women, you change the architecture of my life and the rhythm of my days, and you sneak barefoot into the world of my little affairs, and you close the door behind you, and I do not object."

– A. B.
2025

I stare back at myself in the earthy brown of your eyes; a new and inevitable wave of everything that is you and I crash onto sudden soul
I didn't know that your capable, tangible hands could begin to tread the sandy plains of love in my heart, which I vowed to honor through the waves of time
how can I not adore the grounding earth in your eyes?

We say heart in the same second
we believe divine in the same minute
we feel synergy within the hour

And who knows except God that
we can feel a religious love in a lifetime
that I am capable of knowing love in the seconds my brown eyes lay upon our brushed-up brown noses,
reminiscing love on our brown lands, remembering to forget loss on our brown sand, reminding me to have faith in my brown existence
our bodies come from the same place
the water in our eyes feeds the freedom that we refuse to let go of

And just like that, I, like air caressing one droplet at a time, will move our roots to historic love, I believe in us,

wave after wave,

Friday after Friday,

and lifetime after lifetime.

EARTH

wave after wave Friday after
wave after wave Friday after
wave after wave Friday after
wave after wave Friday after
wave after wave Friday after
wave after wave Friday after
wave after wave Friday after
wave after wave Friday after
wave after wave Friday after
wave after wave Friday after
wave after wave Friday after
wave after wave Friday after
wave after wave Friday after
wave after wave Friday after
wave after wave Friday after
wave after wave Friday after
wave after wave Friday after
wave after wave Friday after
wave after wave Friday after
wave after wave Friday after
wave after wave Friday after
wave after wave Friday after
wave after wave Friday after
wave after wave Friday after
wave after wave Friday after
wave after wave Friday after

Friday and lifetime after lifetime
Friday and lifetime after lifetime
Friday and lifetime after lifetime
Friday and lifetime after lifetime
Friday and lifetime after lifetime
Friday and lifetime after lifetime
Friday and lifetime after lifetime
Friday and lifetime after lifetime
Friday and lifetime after lifetime
Friday and lifetime after lifetime
Friday and lifetime after lifetime
Friday and lifetime after lifetime
Friday and lifetime after lifetime
Friday and lifetime after lifetime
Friday and lifetime after lifetime
Friday and lifetime after lifetime
Friday and lifetime after lifetime
Friday and lifetime after lifetime
Friday and lifetime after lifetime
Friday and lifetime after lifetime
Friday and lifetime after lifetime
Friday and lifetime after lifetime
Friday and lifetime after lifetime
Friday and lifetime after lifetime
Friday and lifetime after lifetime
Friday and lifetime after lifetime

ANGELS

I didn't know what angels who loved me looked like

how their wings moved them around

with the delicateness I've been yearning for

until you walked through my dirt-stained white door

the one with the handle I keep repairing

cracked the door open, wide smile, I know you love me, body and mind

I pray to adore you, your entity, in its entirety, entirely

what I now know is that this is an everlasting thing;

ink onto your heart like how God promises us both heaven and hell

I'm learning what it is to put someone's heart between the aging creases in

my hands I'm terrified of slips; mishaps and misjudgments; betrayal and

deceit it's too easy to claim that you're the sun in my universe, your love must

borrow from the bodies our people have not discovered yet; I love you it's tru

my heart is also an everlasting thing, and I'm an angel too.

BETWEEN THE MOUNTAINS AND THE OCEAN

DIVINE

I talked to our fate through the moon
through what brightens every lover's
sky
I pray to my Creator
that your eyes shine with the good
fortune that could not be given by
anyone except He who put the goodness
in your heart
I pray He protects you and the moon if
I live long enough to see it, to see you,
and to be with you all the way now, and
through to heaven, our perfect fate.

قد أحببتك عبر القمر
عبر ما يضيء سماء كل العاشقين
أدعو لخالقي
أن تتلألأ عينيك بالنور
و تتذكرني عبر البحار
عندما قلبي يدق بمذكرتك

مرت ايامي من قبلي
حبيت و أحببت
و لكن خيالك كان يطوف في عالم بين قلبي و روحي
عالم فارغ كنت افكر به في أعماق الليالي
عالم كان يفوض بدموع كنت اعتقد بان ليس لها لا بداية و لا نهاية و لا نصف
عالم على وشك تدمير نفسه من السؤال
درت في كل جوانب بلادي اتخيلك
و لكن نسيت بان ربي وضعك بين القلب و الروح
كما وضع الشمس في السماء والنبات في الأرض وكل ما بينهما في محله
حبنا شيء لا شك به، بسيط الفهم
و الليالي بدأت تبدو كالنهار في عينيك، الشمس ساطعة في عينيك
خيالك اقتحم كل ما بين قلبي و روحي و بات في عيوني
ولدت في الغرب و انت في الشرق وبين البحار نشأ حبنا

روحـــــي
(MY SOUL)

SEVEN.

THE REBIRTH (OF AN ANCESTRAL DAUGHTER)

“O little light in me, don’t die, /
even if all the galaxies of the world /
close in.”

– Hiba Abu Nada
Not Just Passing
2023

HIBA WAS KILLED BY THE OCCUPATION
ON OCTOBER 20, 2023,
IN KHAN YUNIS, GAZA.

TRANSLATED BY HUDA FAKHREDDINE, 2023.

With an upbeat melody
the grass under me
concrete supporting me
up and down they walk
I don't see but what's up in the sky no clouds in the framed memory
a thunderstorm keeps
mustering up the courage to roar
the tornado is spiraling into silence
almost-icy breeze on my face
with my ears protected
from the distorting sounds
I open my mouth
it is empty
but I am full and meant to be here.

HOPE

THE BUILDUP TO BLISS

Ideal all the time, I am unable to be
thought I could be perfect around the clock
the ticks and the tocks always disagree
I had this static image of myself
of no foul
of no mistakes
now I know I have breathing space
I am allowed to break when my body cannot contain the weight
I am not made to be a perfectly shaped box shipped for convenience
I have the power to leave if you steal the cloud that protects me I will give
forgiveness until I'm misplaced
only because I am made of the sky
from high up, I kill with kindness and leave
I will not apologize for not having enough ammunition, I can't reload
instantly
I will hold hands with time
let it calm the crashing blood within my veins
it's okay if my heart skips a few beats and my mind is overworked the sea will
become static after the storm
I will write prose and poetry that are capable of
soothing my inner workings
I will destroy the demons
with rising above
I am only stardust
on some days I am flying
and on others, I am also beat down
I am made of Adam and Eve
they were bound to fault
it's how they rose from the thorns to the throne this is how I wish to be

I am elevated with light
peace tends to me gently
I will call on existence to carry me
and I will always love endlessly
I grow flowers
some ugly and some beautiful
though they will always be of mesmerizing colors
I protect the flowers on my body
with feeding them words of love and life my growth is mine and no one else's
gently placing me in alternate universes uncreated through soul travelling;
my world is a gift to me
through soul traveling; I go back home
I am a daughter sitting on a bunch of thorns
our moon smiles at me
even when I break
the moon whispers: this is life forevermore, my love
I am everything that builds up to bliss, this is how I wish to be,

AN ANCESTRAL DAUGHTER.

FOOTNOTES

1. I PASS A ROAD CALLED HAIFA ON MOST BUS RIDES I TAKE, AND IT STINGS EVERY TIME. AND BEFORE I TAKE A SECOND TO IMAGINE I AM IN HAIFA, PALESTINE, I LOOK UP AGAIN, AND I AM ON 85TH AVENUE, THE MOST GENERIC NAME A STREET COULD HAVE IN NORTH AMERICA.

2. TATREEZ, ALSO KNOWN AS PALESTINIAN CROSS-STITCHING, HAS USED DIFFERENT MOTIFS AND PATTERNS TO REMEMBER OUR VILLAGES, DISPLACEMENT, AND OUR COLLECTIVE IDENTITY. TATREEZ CAN BE TRACED BACK TO THE 19TH CENTURY.

3. IN REFERENCE TO MOHAMMED EL-KURD'S 2025 BOOK:
"PERFECT VICTIMS AND THE POLITICS OF APPEAL."

4. DEPRESSION, ANXIETY, AND OTHER MENTAL HEALTH DISORDERS AND ISSUES ARE PROMINENT IN GAZA DUE TO THE ONGOING SIEGE AND THE NUMEROUS WARS GAZA HAS SUFFERED FROM SINCE 2008.
REFER TO *"PSYCHOLOGICAL IMPACTS OF THE GAZA WAR ON PALESTINIAN YOUNG ADULTS: A CROSS-SECTIONAL STUDY OF DEPRESSION, ANXIETY, STRESS, AND PTSD SYMPTOMS" BY ALDABBOR ET AL., 2024.*

5. THE ZIONIST PROJECT BUILT A 708-KILOMETER-LONG CONCRETE APARTHEID WALL STARTING IN 1971 TO CONTROL PALESTINIAN MOVEMENT, DIVIDE US, AND MOVE US AWAY FROM OUR LANDS.

6. IN REFERENCE TO "*UNCHILDING*", WHERE THE OCCUPATION FORCES INHUMANE AND UNBEARABLE CONDITIONS ON THE CHILDREN OF PALESTINE, PHYSICALLY AND PSYCHOLOGICALLY FORCING THEM TO GROW UP FASTER, ROBBING THEM OF THEIR CHILDHOOD.

7. THE OCCUPATION HAS COMMITTED ECOCIDE IN GAZA, WHERE THE SOIL AND WATER ARE HARMFUL TO CONSUME AND USE. REFER TO THE UNITED NATIONS'S ARTICLE *"DAMAGE TO GAZA CAUSING NEW RISKS TO HUMAN HEALTH AND LONG-TERM RECOVERY - NEW UNEP ASSESSMENT"* PUBLISHED 2024.

8. IN REFERENCE TO THE ZIONIST PROJECT'S CONSTRUCTION OF WALLS AROUND GAZA. A SANDLINE IS OFTEN USED IN DRILLING.

9. THE OCCUPATION AND ITS SETTLERS BUILT THOUSANDS OF BARS AND CLUBS ON STOLEN LANDS WHERE THEY CONSTANTLY PARTY A FEW KILOMETERS AWAY FROM MURDER IN THE WEST BANK AND GAZA. THIS IS ALSO A REFERENCE TO THE SUPERNOVA FESTIVAL, A PSY-TRANCE BRAZILIAN MUSIC FESTIVAL, WHERE FOREIGN NATIONALS AND

SETTLERS ATTENDING WERE PARTYING AS WELL, 19 KILOMETERS AWAY FROM GAZA.

10. IN REFERENCE TO THE OCCUPATION'S "DESERT INTO AN OASIS" RHETORIC, WHERE THE OCCUPATION UNDERMINES OUR CIVILITY AND PRE-COLONIZATION INFRASTRUCTURE TO JUSTIFY THEIR INNOVATION ON STOLEN LAND.

11. MY FAMILY, SINCE THE MID-19TH CENTURY UNTIL 1948, HAS INHABITED SARAFAND AL-AMAR. BEFORE 1948, AROUND 1,900 PEOPLE INHABITED THE VILLAGE, AND IT HAD 2 ELEMENTARY SCHOOLS. MY VILLAGE IS THE BURIAL PLACE OF ONE OF ITS HISTORICAL INHABITANTS, LUQMAN AL-HAKIM (LUKE THE WISE). ON MAY 19-20, 1948, SARAFAND AL-AMAR WAS OCCUPIED BY THE ZIONIST PROJECT, AND MY FAMILY FLED TO RAFAH, GAZA, WALKING FOR 3 DAYS ON FOOT, CARRYING ALL OF THEIR BELONGINGS ON THEIR BACKS. MY VILLAGE NOW HOUSES ONE OF THE LARGEST MILITARY BASES OF THE OCCUPATION, USED TO KILL THE PEOPLE IN THE CITY MY FAMILY FLED TO. REFER TO WALID KHALIDI'S 1992 BOOK: ALL THAT REMAINS.

12. ON MARCH 5, 2024, THE SPANISH & PORTUGUESE SYNAGOGUE IN MONTREAL, CANADA, HOSTED REAL ESTATE AGENTS WHO WERE ILLEGALLY SELLING PROPERTY

IN PALESTINE. THE QUEBEC SUPERIOR COURT ORDERED AN INJUNCTION AGAINST PROTESTORS THE NEXT DAY, WHERE THEY COULD NOT BE WITHIN 50 METERS OF THE SYNAGOGUE FOR 10 DAYS. REFER TO CTV NEWS' ARTICLE *"COURT INJUNCTION EXTENDED FOR PRO-PALESTINIAN GROUPS PROTESTING OUTSIDE JEWISH INSTITUTIONS IN MONTREAL"*, PUBLISHED IN 2024.

13. IN 1951, THE OCCUPATION ESTABLISHED THE CIVIL DEFENSE LAW, WHERE ALL RESIDENTIAL BUILDINGS IN OCCUPIED PALESTINE MUST HAVE BUNKERS.

14. IT IS KNOWN AMONGST PALESTINIANS, DUE TO THE NATURE OF THE OCCUPATION AND THE MENTAL HEALTH ISSUES THAT AFFECT US, THAT PESSIMISM AS AN ATTITUDE PERSISTS IN OUR DAILY LIVES AS PALESTINIANS.

15. GAZA'S BEACHES ARE HEAVILY POLLUTED DUE TO THE POOR MAINTENANCE OF IT AS A RESULT OF THE SIEGE, THE LACK OF ELECTRICITY TO MANAGE POLLUTION, AND OTHER ISSUES. REFER TO *"SEAWATER POLLUTION RAISES CONCERNS OF WATERBORNE DISEASES AND ENVIRONMENTAL HAZARDS IN THE GAZA STRIP"* PUBLISHED BY OXFAM IN 2018.

16. ON JULY 16, 2014, THE OCCUPATION MURDERED FOUR PALESTINIAN CHILDREN FROM THE SAME FAMILY WHILE THEY WERE PLAYING FOOTBALL ON GAZA'S FISHING BEACH: AHED BAKR (9 YEARS), ZAKARIA BAKR (10 YEARS), MOHAMMED BAKR (11 YEARS), AND ISMAIL BAKR (9 YEARS). A WEEK BEFORE, ON JULY 9, 2014, NINE PALESTINIANS WERE KILLED WATCHING A FIFA WORLD CUP GAME. THE ZIONIST PROJECT HAS KILLED 708 PALESTINIAN ATHLETES IN GAZA SINCE OCTOBER 7, 2023 (PALESTINIAN SPORTS MEDIA ASSOCIATION, 2025).

17. ON JULY 9, 2024 (10 YEARS AFTER), THE OCCUPATION KILLED AT LEAST 30 PALESTINIANS AND WOUNDED 53 WHEN THEY BOMBED AL-AWDAH SCHOOL IN KHAN YUNIS, WHICH WAS SERVING AS A SHELTER. REFER TO AL-JAZEERA'S ARTICLE *"ISRAEL BOMBS GAZA SCHOOL, KILLING 30 PALESTINIANS AS TRUCE TALKS CONTINUE"* PUBLISHED 2024.

18. IN REFERENCE TO THE 1973 OCTOBER WAR BETWEEN EGYPT AND THE OCCUPATION.

19. THE ZIONIST PROJECT DESECRATED AT LEAST 16 CEMETERIES IN GAZA, WHERE MANY OF MY FAMILY'S LOVED ONES REST. REFER TO CNN'S ARTICLE *"AT LEAST 16 CEMETERIES IN GAZA HAVE BEEN DESECRATED BY ISRAELI FORCES, SATELLITE IMAGERY AND VIDEOS REVEAL"* PUBLISHED 2024.

20. HUNDREDS OF THOUSANDS OF PALESTINIANS OF DIFFERENT CITIZENSHIP LIVE IN THE GULF STATES. I LIVED IN KUWAIT FOR HALF OF MY LIFE, WHERE THE BIGGEST PALESTINIAN DIASPORA IN THE GULF EXISTS DUE TO A LARGE WAVE OF IMMIGRATION IN THE EARLY YEARS OF THE OCCUPATION.

21. KAZEM, AN ICE CREAM SHOP, IS ONE OF MY FONDEST MEMORIES FROM GAZA. WATCH THE NATIONAL NEWS' 2025 VIDEO REPORT: *"GAZA ICE CREAM SHOP REOPENS, BRINGING HOPE AND RESILIENCE AFTER WAR."*

22. THOUSANDS OF GAZANS GET STUNG BY JELLYFISH PER YEAR, AS JELLYFISH ARE VERY COMMON IN GAZA'S PART OF THE MEDITERRANEAN SEA, AND MOST GAZANS CAN EASILY REMEDY THE STING. REFER TO HAMIDA AND ABDALLAH'S 2025 PUBLICATION: *"JELLYFISH SPECIES RECORDED IN THE MEDITERRANEAN ECOSYSTEM OF THE GAZA STRIP, PALESTINE."*

23. SINCE THE OCCUPATION'S SIEGE ON GAZA AND EVEN BEFORE THE CURRENT GENOCIDE, GAZANS FACED MANY ELECTRICITY ISSUES THROUGHOUT THE YEAR. REFER TO HAMMOUDA'S 2023 PUBLICATION: *"THE ELECTRICITY SECTOR IN PALESTINE: TOWARDS LESS DEPENDENCE ON ISRAEL."*

www.ingramcontent.com/pod-product-compliance
Lightning Source LLC
LaVergne TN
LVHW010606110826
845149LV00003B/785

* 9 7 8 1 9 9 8 3 0 9 6 3 4 *